SECOND NATURE
CHANGES & CHALLENGES IN THE NEW ENVIRONMENT

Word of Mouth

THE FOOD YOU EAT

By Nancy Rogers Bontempo
with Mark Stewart

NORWOODHOUSE PRESS

All images courtesy of Getty Images, except for the following:
Deposit Photos (6, 14, 22, 26, 32, 40, 41 & 44); Yue Jin, Cereal Disease Laboratory (8); Bartlett's
Ocean View Farm (16); Dr. Phil Brown (18); Black Book Partners archives (21, 36); Brian Llewellyn
Smith (24); Global Crop Diversity Trust (27 & 42); Post Oak RC&D Area (31); The Land Institute
(34); Stonyfield Farm (35 top); Jae-hyun Kim (35 bottom); Michigan State University (43).

Cover: Mahmud Hams/AFP/Getty Images

Special thanks to Content Consultant Ashley McDowell.

Copyright © 2012 by Norwood House Press

Library of Congress Cataloging-in-Publication Data

Bontempo, Nancy Rogers.
  Word of mouth : the food you eat / By Nancy Rogers Bontempo, Mark Stewart.
     p. cm. -- (Second nature)
  Includes bibliographical references and index.
  Summary: "One billion people on the planet do not get enough food every
day. This book explores why this is everyone's problem, and helps readers
understand how the global food supply is connected to environmental stress,
as well as the science behind ensuring that food is safe and plentiful. An
emphasis is placed on worldwide agricultural practices and
innovations"--Provided by publisher.
  ISBN-13: 978-1-59953-449-7 (library edition : alk. paper)
  ISBN-10: 1-59953-449-5 (library edition : alk. paper)
1. Food supply--Juvenile literature. 2. Agriculture--Social
aspects--Juvenile literature. I. Stewart, Mark, 1960- II. Title.
  HD9000.5.B524 2012
  338.1'9--dc23
                        2011017619

Manufactured in the United States of America in North Mankato, Minnesota.
176N—072011

COVER: A hand holds freshly harvested olives. Feeding all of the world's hungry people is one of our most pressing challenges.

Contents

Words in **bold** type are defined on page 46.

What's the Problem?

One billion people on this planet are undernourished. In other words, they do not get enough food every day of their lives. At first, you might think, *That's not really my problem*—especially if you live in the United States. Actually, it is. Of all the things that make people do desperate things, hunger is at the very top of the list. It strikes everywhere, including the U.S. And when a billion people are desperate, it is bound to affect you—no matter where you live.

The stories in these pages look at the relationship among food, community, and the environment. They also take into account the bigger picture of human activity. As you will see, the way people live and the decisions they make have an effect on the world's food supply.

We have been searching for solutions to our food needs for thousands and thousands of years. Humans began

For this mother in Africa, putting food on the table is a daily struggle. This is the case for millions around the world, including people in the United States.

In places where food is plentiful, it is easy to forget that we may soon face serious shortages.

eating meat more than two million years ago. Past cultures developed planting and farming techniques in places all around the world as early as 7,000 B.C. The abundance of food helped communities grow and created important social bonds and **rituals**. From one century to the next, people experimented with new ways to grow crops and raise animals to feed the ever-increasing population. That work continues today. It is more important than ever because there are more humans on the planet than ever.

In 2011, the world population reached 7 billion. By the time people your age have children and they finish school, there may be more than 9 billion people in the world. That is an increase of more than 25 percent. And because the diets of people in large countries such as China and India are improving, the amount of **calories** the world will consume will probably rise by 50 percent. With more mouths to feed, more nutritious (and better) food must be produced.

If it isn't, the hunger problem will grow. This could have a direct impact on you. For example, countries weakened by food shortages can become unsteady and affect the world's balance of power. People who don't get proper nutrition are more likely to get diseases that could be passed on to others.

At the same time, the world will need places for people to live. That means the amount of land available to grow food will probably shrink. Also, because humans continue to create more waste, the risk posed by pollution is likely to grow. And don't forget—people will be using more energy, which may add to the pollution problem.

Food Stress

In 2011, North Africa and the Middle East became the focus of much of the world's attention. Unrest in this region toppled cruel dictators. It was an exciting and happy time for millions of people. Afterwards, the new governments faced great challenges. One of the biggest problems was making sure that people could get enough food.

What is at stake? If these countries cannot feed their citizens, people will simply go somewhere else to live. Over the next 10 years, "food stress" could cause 50 million people in this region to move to places where there is more to eat. For most, the shortest trip is to Southern Europe, including Spain, Italy, and France.

Food Security

In 1998, farmers in the African country of Uganda noticed that something was attacking the stems of their wheat plants. This problem soon spread to neighboring countries and then "jumped" to parts of Western Asia. Wheat farmers in Australia and North and South America are bracing themselves for the day it arrives in their fields.

The culprit is called Ug99. It stands for Uganda and 1999, the year the problem was identified. Ug99 is a **fungus** that causes "stem rust." Researchers are racing to find a way to control the fungus. In 2011, billionaire Bill Gates donated $70 million to support "food security" around the world. Ug99 was on the top of his list of problems to address.

What is the challenge scientists face in battling Ug99? Wheat grows in many different climates. That means a different solution may be necessary to fight the fungus in each climate. In the meantime, the fungus may evolve into new strains that will continue to attack food supplies.

The Ug99 fungus attacks the stems of wheat plants.

THE FORCE OF FIVE

Population growth is one of five major forces that put stress on the world food supply. The others are **climate change**, natural enemies, pollution, and poor farming techniques. Each has an impact on the others—and on you.

Climate change happens as a result of the environment's natural cycles as well as human activity. It affects the food supply in several ways. The world appears to be getting warmer. No one can say for sure how much of **global warming** is due to human activity, or how much worse it will get. One thing scientists agree on is that no one has figured out a good way of reversing climate change.

Fluctuating temperatures affect agriculture in several ways. Plants and animals that flourish in one climate do not always do well in another. Changing temperatures tend to trigger unpredictable weather, which also has an impact on the food supply. Warmer temperatures may create opportunities for natural enemies or "pests" to damage food supplies. These pests include animals, insects, and microorganisms.

To meet these challenges, some people will rely on "old" solutions. They will use more chemicals to increase the food supply and more **pesticides** to protect it. Some of these products are bad for people and the environment.

Poor farming techniques, such as "slash-and-burn" agriculture, could also move us close to an environmental catastrophe. The term slash-and-burn refers to clearing forests by cutting down trees and burning them. This technique can do great harm to **ecosystems** and make it even harder to feed the world. When ecosystems are thrown into disarray, a ripple effect can take place. An environmental change in one part of the world can eventually be felt in another part.

Not all old solutions are harmful. People developed them based on the best information available at the time, and many still work very well. But that does not mean we should stop looking for new answers. Our search must keep moving forward. Environmental scientists hope that more people will take an interest in this problem, especially children and teenagers. That is the best way to create the momentum needed to find solutions.

LEFT: Pilgrim crickets feast on wheat plants. These insects have found ways to resist pesticides.
ABOVE: Only charred brush remains after slash-and-burn farmers cleared this land.

WORLD VIEW

Hunger is defined in many ways, but everyone from scientists to politicians agrees that roughly a billion people don't get enough food. According to the United Nations Food and Agriculture Organization, there were 926 million hungry people around the world in 2010.

Total = 926 million hungry people

- Developed Countries: 19 million (2%)
- Near East and North Africa: 37 million (4%)
- Latin America and the Caribbean: 53 million (6%)
- Sub-Saharan Africa: 239 million (26%)
- Asia and the Pacific: 578 million (62%)

How We Got Here

HARD LESSONS ABOUT THE FOOD WE EAT

A person living in the United States in the 1800s would be amazed to walk through a modern-day grocery store. Back then, only the wealthiest people could ever hope to afford such a wide selection of food. Many people in northern climates never got the chance to taste tropical fruits such as bananas. Farmers ate what they raised, but farm life could be very unpredictable. In many parts of the country—and the rest of the world—people survived on bread and stew. (And you could never be sure what was in the stew!)

What those long-ago people might find very familiar are the questions we ask about the food we eat today. Is it clean? Is it safe? Is it healthy?

No one living in the 1800s—not even the wealthy—could have imagined shopping in a grocery store with this much fresh food.

Before stores had refrigerators, food such as meat, fish, and fowl often spoiled before it was sold. Store-bought fruit and vegetables did not look or taste the way they do today. Grocers ordered produce before it was ripe, hoping that it would last a long time on the shelves. It did not. And it tasted terrible. Also, some people believed that fruit spread a disease called cholera. Cholera is caused by **bacteria** in drinking water and sometimes in seafood. Before the disease was understood, many people avoided fruit altogether.

THE MILK MYSTERY

Milk was considered to be the healthiest of drinks in the 1800s. But one glass of milk could taste very different

A milkman makes a delivery in the early 1900s.
The milk was fresh, but was it safe?

from the next. It was common for milk sellers to add water in order to increase the amount they could sell. When they wanted to "thicken" the milk-water mixture, they sometimes added chalk or plaster.

Milk from a farm tasted much better, but it was not always safe to drink. Cities often sold their garbage to farmers, who fed it to their pigs. Some also fed it to their cows. The bacteria in the garbage came back to the cities in the milk, causing people to get sick. **Tuberculosis** was one of the deadly diseases that could be transmitted by a sick cow. Because children drank a lot of milk, many fell ill and died. Fortunately, this is not the case today.

Until recently, scientists believed that cows were solely to blame for tuberculosis. But a study in 2008 showed that humans gave tuberculosis to

The Role of the FDA

Food testing is a vital part of the food supply chain. For example, in the 1800s, some dishonest grocers sold their customers a mixture of animal fat, water, and potatoes and labeled it "butter." Without a system in place to test food products, no one knew about this practice. In 1906, the Food and Drug Administration (FDA) was formed by President Theodore Roosevelt to protect people. Today, the FDA has strict standards for what goes into foods.

Does that mean the days of bad butter are over? In 2010, tests on one company's butter showed a high level of a chemical that is supposed to be used for fireproofing. Scientists studied the problem, which they knew was not caused on purpose. They eventually found the culprit—it was the wrapper around the butter.

cows thousands of years ago. Cows just gave it back. This shows that there is still much we do not understand about food safety.

THE NEED FOR VARIETY

One thing we do know is that people who depend on one type of food—either to eat or to sell—are always at risk. In the 1800s, the potato crop in Ireland was destroyed by a **blight**. Not only did the plants die, the blight filled the air with a disgusting smell. Facing starvation, people left Ireland in large numbers and fled to the United States.

Millions of Irish-Americans can trace their roots back to these immigrants. What they may not realize is that the plant that "drove" them across the Atlantic Ocean originally came to Europe from the Americas. Early explorers returning home brought potatoes with them. They found that the potato grew extremely well in European soil. With more food to eat, people could have larger families, and populations swelled. When the potatoes died in Ireland, people had to find a country that could feed them.

The famine that began on Irish farms such as this one drove around one million starving people across the Atlantic Ocean.

Today, scientists are still worried about what people will do when the food they depend on starts to disappear through disease, climate change, or overpopulation. In Africa, the **cassava**—a root plant that supplies important calories—is threatened by blight. Millions rely on cassavas. Where will they go if the problem is not solved?

LEARNING FROM BANANAS

Today, our meat may be fresher, our produce riper, and our milk cleaner. However, when it comes to the long-term impact of altering ecosystems, there is a lot more we have to learn. Take the banana, for example. Almost all of the bananas sold in stores worldwide are called Cavendish bananas. They are originally from China. More than any other type of banana, the Cavendish has the size, flavor, vitamins, texture, and thick skin that make it perfect to ship all over the world. This type of banana also ripens slowly and doesn't bruise easily. Americans eat more than 7 billion bananas a year—99 percent are Cavendish and almost all are grown in Central and South America.

Does anyone rely solely on bananas to survive? Probably not, but a lot of people could not survive without the jobs that banana farming provides. Several years ago, a disease wiped out the Cavendish banana in Asia. The killer was a fungus that grows in the soil. It spreads easily and cannot be killed by chemicals. Scientists tried to **crossbreed** a Cavendish banana resistant to the fungus, but they failed. If the disease crosses the Pacific Ocean, the bananas we now take for granted may become a distant memory. Worse, millions of people in Central and South America may have to find new jobs—or another place to live. That could lead to more people crossing into the United States illegally.

How did we reach this point? In the case of the Cavendish, it is because banana growers created a "monoculture." This meant that they relied so heavily on one type of plant that they put their entire industry at risk if something went wrong. They did so because the Cavendish was the most profitable banana to grow and sell—even though they knew that there might be problems with their lack of variety.

When a company clears miles and miles of jungle to plant one specific crop, it enables that crop's enemies to grow stronger and do more damage. This type of monoculture may also eliminate the things that keep that enemy in check. The creation of large banana plantations in Central and South America has given us inexpensive fruit in great abundance. However, it may have come at a very high price.

WIPED OUT

Long before the Cavendish banana made it to grocery stores, there was the Gros Michel banana (right). During the early 1900s, this was the banana that the world ate and loved. The company we know today as Chiquita Banana grew rich selling the Gros Michel. So did other fruit companies. When disease began threatening their bananas in the 1920s, they were slow to react. They did not understand the environmental impact of their growing practices. By 1970, disease had wiped out the Gros Michel.

3 If We Do Nothing

WILL OUR FOOD CHALLENGES GO AWAY?

Anyone who has faced a tricky problem knows that the easy thing to do is put it off until later. Sometimes we want to ask the advice of others. Sometimes we wait until we have time to focus fully on a solution. Often a problem is best solved after we step back and think about different options. When our food supply is at risk, these are not always good reasons to wait. The world's population grows every day. If there is less food available, then people starve. Failing to act effectively and soon may cost lives.

GROWING PROBLEMS

Two of the greatest challenges when it comes to feeding people are linked to much bigger environmental issues: climate change and land use. Most scientists agree that the earth's climate is heating up and that the burning of fossil fuels such as gasoline and coal is a major part of this problem. One outcome of burning these fuels is the release of **carbon dioxide**. Carbon dioxide is a greenhouse gas—a gas that traps heat in the atmosphere, just as a greenhouse does during the winter. Today the amount of carbon dioxide

In dry climates, growing food becomes almost impossible as the temperature rises.

NOT SO FAST

In 2006, scientists began talking about slowing down global warming by blocking sunlight. One idea was to release sulfur dioxide into the atmosphere. This gas would mix with water and reflect some of the sun's rays back into space. People liked this idea until other scientists pointed out that it might cool down the land faster than the oceans. This would weaken the summer **monsoons** that bring nourishing rain to Asia and Africa—and in turn create a worldwide food shortage. In this case, moving too quickly to solve an environmental problem might have created an even bigger one.

The monsoon season in parts of Asia creates excellent growing conditions.

in the atmosphere is almost 400 parts per million. A century ago it was under 300 parts per million. That's a big difference.

When the temperature changes in a place where food grows, it can trigger a number of other changes. There may be more or less water reaching farms either from rain or from rivers. Seeds may sprout too early or too late, and plants may not grow to the same size that they normally do. There may be a change in the number of insects that help **fertilize** crops, as well as the number of insects that attack crops. Blights that were easily controlled can get out of control.

Climate shifts affect organisms in the sea, too. For example, a slight change in ocean temperature can disrupt the marine food chain. The result is that the number of fish that reach our tables may fall. Once again, a problem that seems far removed from you can have a real impact on your life.

USING LAND EFFECTIVELY

Land use is another tricky problem. Every year, as the world population grows, people move onto land that had been used to grow and raise food. To feed more people with less land, we must be smarter about how we use the land. In **industrialized** countries such as the United States, modern technology has helped solve this problem by making food production more efficient. These solutions include better farming techniques and more effective uses of water. But they may not work in poorer countries where technology lags behind. Sadly, it is in these places that population is growing the fastest and the need for food is greatest.

Environmental scientists have their hands full. There are parts of the world—including places in Africa and Asia— where agricultural techniques have remained the same for centuries. That means that people have not adapted to changes in the environment, which could make their farming practices less effective. Why does this matter to you? The United States is a generous country that often reaches out to people in need, especially those struck by natural disasters. If we focus more attention on helping foreign countries meet their food demands, we may have fewer resources available to address our own challenges.

FRUITS OF THEIR LABOR

As populations expand and the need for food increases, we must find more plants that are nutritious and easy to grow. While food scientists are working on new ways to meet this demand, **botanists** are looking at an old friend: breadfruit.

Breadfruit is rich in **protein**, **fiber**, and **carbohydrates**. It's a good source of energy and tastes a little like a potato. It also grows very fast. More than 200 years ago, British scientists brought the plant to the Caribbean from the Pacific Islands. Breadfruit did well in the humidity of the Caribbean islands. However, it was hard to grow in other environments.

In 2009, researchers in Hawaii found ways to make breadfruit adapt to varied climates. Those include regions at higher elevations with less rainfall and different types of soil. Scientists now believe breadfruit can do well in Central America and Africa, where hunger is especially bad.

Food scientists hope that breadfruit will help solve world hunger.

THE SVALBARD GLOBAL SEED VAULT

When you are told that a museum's art collection is "priceless," it means that the paintings on display could not be replaced at any cost. What is the world's most valuable collection? It's not art. It's seeds.

The Svalbard Global Seed Vault (below)—built underground in a remote area of Norway—holds samples of millions of plant seeds. They are kept dry and cool just in case a species is wiped out by disease, insects, or a natural disaster.

Stored correctly, a seed can last for thousands of years. If the Svalbard Global Seed Vault should lose power, the seeds would still be good for centuries because of the cold climate. No one can say for sure how or when the seeds will be needed. However, environmental scientists agree that not having the vault would be like running a supercomputer without a backup disk.

4 Bright Ideas

NEW WAYS TO FEED THE WORLD

When environmental scientists look at the world's food situation, they worry. The questions are so complicated and, for most people, the answers are either too hard to understand or too expensive to afford. That doesn't stop the scientific community from putting ideas to work. Waiting for the "big changes" to come may be frustrating, but it doesn't mean you can't start making small changes.

The people working at the International Rice Research Institute (IRRI) know how small changes can make a big impact. Fifty years ago, they helped develop a type of rice that produced much bigger harvests. Asian countries that had once spent a lot of time and money feeding their people were able to focus their attention elsewhere. The result was amazing growth in the region's business opportunities and also its population.

A woman in Asia works the rice harvest. Improving the quality of crops can help decrease the number of hungry people in the world.

Now the IRRI has been called upon to make another miracle. With predictions of extreme weather patterns due to climate change, Asia's rice crop might be threatened in the future. The same could be true in Africa and South America. The IRRI is in a race to create new kinds of rice strong enough to withstand floods and droughts. They are having good luck with a variety that can even grow on dry land. These new types of rice will also help struggling farmers who are trying to grow rice in poor conditions today.

SUSTAINABLE AGRICULTURE

A term you hear more and more is "sustainable agriculture." Mostly it is used to describe a way of raising food that does not cause too much stress on the environment. This practice helps sustain the surrounding population and ecosystems. For example, people have known for centuries that plowed land blows or washes away about five times faster than new soil builds up. This process is called erosion. In places where farming has been going on for centuries, there is not much good soil left.

Can you grow crops without plowing the land each year? Yes, through a technique called "no-till" farming. Instead of turning over the soil, seeds are planted with a special drill. Besides slowing erosion, no-till farming has other benefits. It keeps helpful organisms (including earthworms) from being destroyed and uses less water. It is also less expensive.

No-till farming is gaining popularity in the United States. The rest of the world has to catch up—right now just over 5 percent of farming is done this way around the globe. One hope is for industries to give money to countries to encourage this type of sustainable agriculture.

In the process, the amount of pollution caused by farming would be slowly reduced as well. The soil in plowed fields releases a lot of carbon dioxide into the air. No-till fields release hardly any. In the United States, where carbon dioxide **emissions** are a major problem, this would help make the air you breathe cleaner.

GRASS-FED CATTLE

Another type of sustainable agriculture can be found at more than 1,000 ranches around the United States. They differ from other ranches because they let their cattle graze in open pastures. You may not realize it, but most of the beef that ends up on the dinner table and in the drive-thru is raised in feed lots.

Cattle in feed lots are given soy and grain that were grown with pesticides. Also, the animals are injected with drugs that keep them from getting sick and help them grow faster. Grass-fed cattle **forage** for food and are moved

Raising cattle on a grass diet is good for the earth and produces more nutritious beef.

from one field to another when the grass is at its most nutritious. People who eat meat can tell the difference. Grass-fed beef has less fat than feed-lot beef and more of vitamins A and E.

How does raising cattle on grass help the environment? Grass grows naturally, needing little help from humans. On the other hand, many of the products used to fatten cattle in feed lots could be used to feed people. Or at least, the land used to raise cattle feed could be planted with more beneficial crops.

The greatest benefit of grass-fed cattle to the human race may be that ranchers need little or no antibiotics to keep their animals healthy. Antibiotics are medicines that control bacteria. The overuse of antibiotics has created bacteria that are resistant to medicine. These bacteria play a part in the deaths of nearly 100,000 people a year.

Keep it Simple

Sometimes, the best solutions to the planet's food problems are the simplest ones. A group called Doctors Without Borders (DWB) has proven this to be true. DWB helps people all over the world who are poor and hungry. To feed starving children, the organization distributes a mixture of peanut butter and milk powder called Plumpy'nut. It was invented by a famous nutritionist named André Briend. Plumpy'nut is served in foil packages that look like ketchup packs. That makes it easy to transport.

Plumpy'nut provides important vitamins and minerals. Kids gain weight and become healthier when they eat it. With this idea in mind, similar foods are being developed to treat children suffering from **malnutrition**.

Children in Ethiopia are among those who rely on Plumpy'nut for nutrition.

5 Trailblazers

These people are doing things to help feed the world today…and make the world better for tomorrow.

GARY HIRSHBERG
Yogurt King

Can a company make a lot of money without hurting the planet? Until Hirshberg (left) came along, no one knew for sure. But Stonyfield Yogurt proved it could be done by being completely **organic**, reducing greenhouse gases, limiting the amount of water it uses, and turning its discarded yogurt into biogas. Stonyfield was also the first American company to offset 100 percent of its carbon dioxide emissions.

WES JACKSON
Geneticist

Jackson is leading a team of researchers at The Land Institute in Salina, Kansas. They hope to create a "perennial" grain. Perennial plants come back year after year and use water very efficiently. If Jackson is successful in making a perennial version of wheat or barley, it will save farmers time and money—and be easier on the earth, too.

LEE CHONG BOUN

Farmer

Several years ago, Boun (right) quit the sneaker business in South Korea to become an apple farmer. Why did he change careers? He found a way to grow square apples in plastic containers. Because the apples pack neatly together, they take up less space during shipping. That is good for the environment because less fuel is burned per apple on the way to the store.

AMY SMITH

Engineer

Smith is a professor at the Massachusetts Institute of Technology (MIT). She designs simple machines that can be made and used by people in the poorest parts of the world. One of Smith's greatest inventions is a mill that turns grain into flour quickly and easily. She has inspired her MIT students to follow in her footsteps.

6 Field Tested

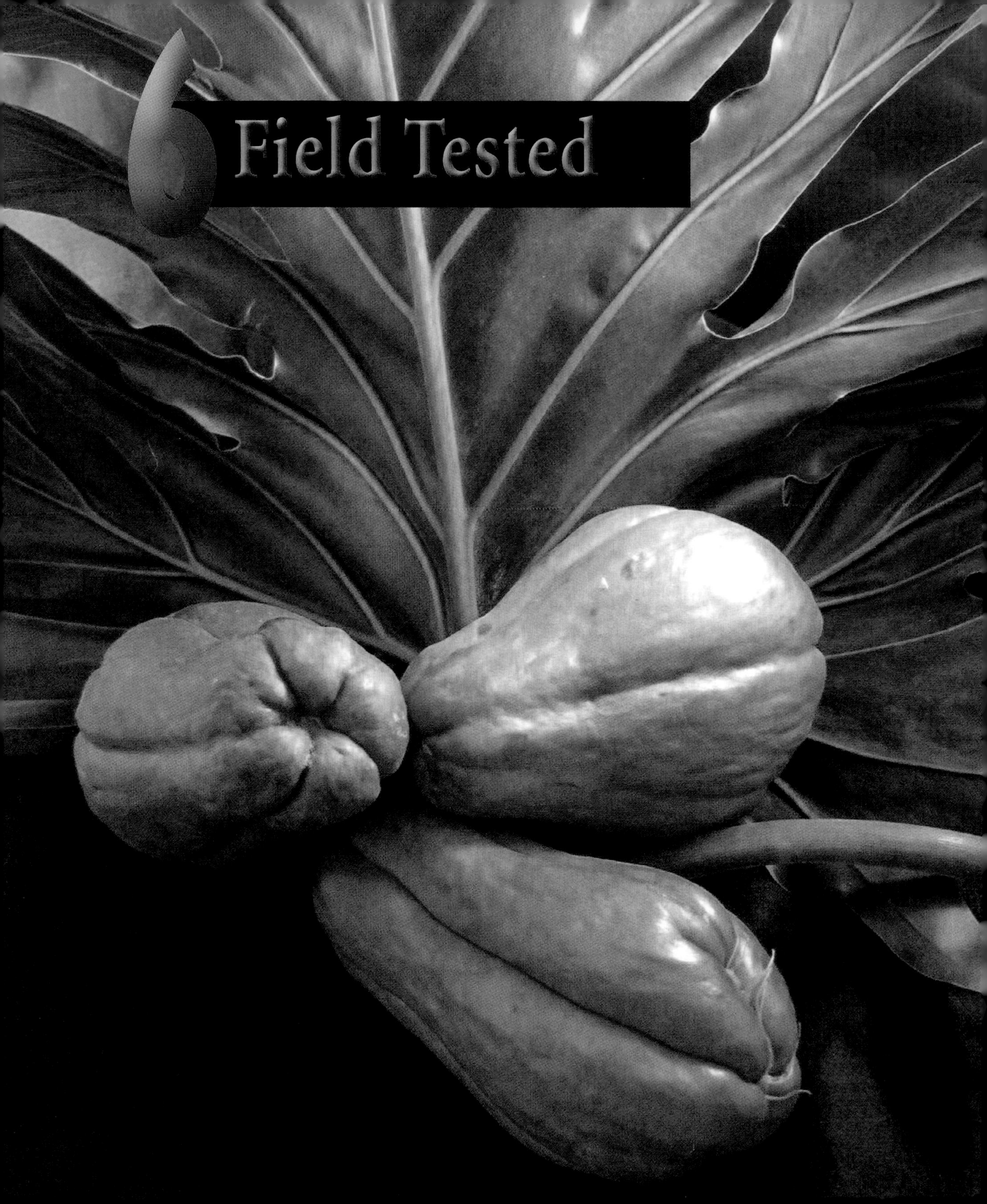

n the drizzly forests of Asia, Central America, and Australia, one of the most abundant plants is the chayote. Its wrinkled, pear-shaped fruit tastes like a cross between a potato and a cucumber. It is a very good source of **amino acids** and vitamin C. It can be cooked like squash or sliced right onto a salad.

Outside of these wet, wild areas, the chayote is hardly known. That may be changing soon. Scientists have been working to produce a variety that can grow in dryer, cooler climates. The trick is to do so without losing the crisp, satisfying flavor that makes the chayote a favorite of people in its native environments.

One company in Israel has developed a variety of chayote that holds much promise. It could grow on farms in most agricultural regions of the world. While the new chayote won't solve hunger problems all by itself, it is a step in the right direction. Chayote also has added health benefits. Potato lovers can get the same flavor and fullness in a chayote, with 75 percent fewer calories.

The chayote may not look glamorous, but it is delicious and nutritious—and it could be an effective weapon in the war on hunger.

Career Opportunities

WORKING TO SOLVE
OUR FOOD CHALLENGES

When it comes to jobs in the food industry, there are lots of choices. Biologists and chemists working with agricultural engineers have a tremendous responsibility. They must come up with ideas on how to create more food out of existing land and resources.

Because it is expensive to move food from one place to another, many food scientists are studying ways for people to grow and manufacture everything they need a short distance from where they live. If researchers are successful, it will help prevent massive population movement created by food stress.

A team of scientists in South Korea cuts open a piece of beef. Studying different aspects of food can lead to solutions to hunger problems.

This picture shows *Salmonella* at the microscopic level.

Sometimes food scientists must act as detectives. Often, they are on the trail of *Salmonella*, a bacteria that can survive and grow on eggs, meat, nuts, and other everyday foods. *Salmonella* is unusual because it does well in very dry and very wet environments. Other bacteria grow only where there is moisture. When people eat foods with *Salmonella*, they get very ill. Some even die.

When *Salmonella* was found in peanut butter in 2009, food scientists spent hundreds of hours and traveled thousands of miles trying to trace the problem back to its source. They made sure that all the contaminated peanut butter was taken off the shelves of grocery stores. The company responsible for the faulty product was forced to look at its business practices and correct any mistakes.

TINY FACTORIES

Biologists working to understand **microbes** have some exciting options. Microbes are like little chemical factories. They run on two things that are in ample supply: garbage and moisture.

We are just beginning to unlock the potential of microbes. One exciting use is putting them to work replacing traditional chemical pesticides. Insects have grown resistant to many chemical pesticides. Meanwhile, these same chemicals are showing up in our food, affecting our health and damaging the environment. A microbe called *Bacillus thurengiensis* has been used for years to kill insects that destroy shrubs, trees, and forests. Imagine the benefits if scientists can find a way to get microbes to protect crops from their natural enemies!

GROWING SOLUTION

Chances are, there will always be populations that cannot feed themselves properly. That is why many food scientists are working on nutritional supplements to make up the difference. One answer may be algae—a food source that is already very popular in Asia.

There are hundreds of types of algae. If you have ever had a sushi roll (right) or miso soup in a Japanese restaurant, you've probably eaten it—seaweed is a type of algae. In China, more than 50 different kinds are available. Algae is packed with vitamins and is rich in calcium, iodine, iron, magnesium, and potassium.

The natural oil from algae is very good for you, too. In fact, the healthy oil in fish (omega-3 fatty acid) starts as algae in the ocean, where it is part of the marine food chain.

8 Expert Opinions

When the best minds talk about the world's food supply, it's worth listening to what they say...

"If you think of it as an insurance policy for the world, you can't beat the value."

>—*Cary Fowler, executive director of the Global Crop Diversity Trust, on the $9 million price tag for the Svalbard Global Seed Vault*

"Don't eat anything your great-grandmother wouldn't recognize as food."

>—*Michael Pollan, food writer, on his personal rule about eating processed food*

"Few things make you feel better about your health than eating organic fruits and veggies."

>—*Dr. Sanjay Gupta, health expert, on the best reason to "go organic"*

"It was food shortages that put people in Tunisia and Egypt over the top."
— *Ewen Todd, Michigan State University professor, on how he believes food stress led people in North Africa to topple their governments*

"It's not an issue of not having enough food...do we have enough food to go around? Yes. But do we distribute it equitably? At this point, definitely not."
— *Julia Lee, University of Toronto professor, on the problem of getting food to the people who need it*

"Everyone freaks out and figures you must be hurting the tree. I don't know where they think maple syrup comes from!"
— *Ava Chin, food writer, on the reaction of neighbors when she taps the maple tree outside her New York apartment building*

LEFT: Cary Fowler   ABOVE: Ewen Todd

9 What Can I Do?

Have you ever heard of a locavore? That is what people who eat only locally grown food call themselves. They are part of a movement that began in the United States. Locavores shop for their fruits, vegetables, meat, and dairy products in farmers markets. By supporting local companies—and by turning away from foods grown abroad or shipped over long distances—locavores support sustainable agriculture in the places they live.

When locavores go to the grocery store, they check labels carefully to see where food comes from. In the typical shopping cart, the average distance food travels to market can be more than 1,500 miles. It takes a lot of fuel to move food that distance.

Most locavores make exceptions for some foods, such as coffee and tropical fruit, which do not grow well in the U.S. Sometimes, locavores will pick a month and try a 100-mile or 200-mile diet. That means everything they eat and drink cannot come from farther away than that distance.

You can be part of the sustainability movement by thinking like a locavore. Pick a week and convince your family to try a 500-mile diet. It takes great discipline and a keen eye, but it can be done. Even if you have to break the rules on one or two items, you'll eat healthier and have fun.

Becoming a locavore—and even growing your own vegetables—is a fun way to make your corner of the world a healthier place.

Glossary

Amino Acids—Molecules that are the building blocks of proteins.

Bacteria—Single-celled organisms that live in soil, water, or bodies of plants and animals.

Blight—Any type of disease that can wipe out crops or other plants.

Botanists—People who study plants and flowers.

Calories—Units that measure how much energy is produced by food.

Carbohydrates—Compounds of carbon, hydrogen, and oxygen formed by green plants. Carbohydrates are an important energy source for humans.

Carbon Dioxide—A colorless gas made up of one part carbon and two parts oxygen.

Cassava—A plant grown in tropical climates that produces a nutritious starch.

Climate Change—A long-term change in weather conditions.

Crossbreed—Combine two different breeds or species to produce a new variety.

Ecosystems—All the organisms, plants, and animals that make up specific ecological areas.

Emissions—Substances discharged into the air.

Fertilize—Add nutrients to soil to help plants grow.

Fiber—The part of plant food that helps the human body expel waste.

Forage—Search for food.

Fungus—Organisms that grow on other organisms. Mold, mildew, and stem rust are types of fungus.

Global Warming—An increase in the earth's temperature caused by increases in greenhouse gases. There is debate among scientists about how much of global warming is caused by human activity.

Industrialized—Dependent on factories, businesses, and agriculture to create jobs and revenues.

Malnutrition—Not getting enough nutrients to feed the body.

Microbes—Another term for microorganisms or germs.

Monsoons—Periods of extremely heavy rainfall.

Organic—Produced naturally, without the help of pesticides or chemical fertilizers.

Pesticides—Chemicals used to kill bugs that feed on crops.

Protein—A substance in foods that gives the body vital nutrients.

Rituals—Actions that are always performed in the same order.

Tuberculosis—A disease that attacks the lungs.

Sources

The authors relied on many different books, magazines, and organizations to do research for this book. Listed below are the primary sources of information and their websites:

The Associated Press	www.ap.org
Canadian Broadcasting Corporation	www.cbc.ca
National Agricultural Library	www.nal.usda.gov
National Geographic Magazine	www.nationalgeographic.com
The New York Times	www.nytimes.com
The New Yorker Magazine	www.newyorker.com
Newsweek Magazine	www.newsweek.com
Science Magazine	www.sciencemag.org
Seed Magazine	www.seedmagazine.com
Time Magazine	www.time.com
U.S. Food and Drug Administration	www.fda.gov

Resources

To get involved with efforts to help the environment, you can contact these organizations:

American Association for the Advancement of Science	www.aaas.org
The Global Crop Diversity Trust	www.croptrust.org
United Nations World Food Programme	www.wfp.org

For more information on the subjects covered in this book:

Chancellor, Deborah. *Science Kids: Planet Earth.* New York, New York. Kingfisher, 2008.

Cherry, Lynne, and Braasch, Gary. *How We Know What We Know About Our Changing Climate: Scientists and Kids Explore Global Warming.* Nevada City, California. Dawn Publications, 2008.

Juettner, Bonnie. *The Seed Vault.* Chicago, Illinois. Norwood House Press, 2010.

Taylor-Butler, Christine. *Food Safety.* Danbury, Connecticut. Children's Press, 2008.

Index

Page numbers in **bold** refer to illustrations.

The Authors

DR. NANCY ROGERS BONTEMPO is a food microbiologist with a Ph.D. from Rutgers University. Nancy works for Kraft Foods in Food Safety and Microbiology. She divides her time between labwork and fieldwork. In 2009, Nancy's sleuthing helped prevent a *Salmonella* outbreak in nut products.

MARK STEWART has written more than 200 non-fiction books for the school and library market. He has an undergraduate degree in History from Duke University. Mark's work in environmental studies includes books on the plants and animals of New York (where he grew up) and New Jersey (where he lives now).